DEVOUT

Hadley Jones

Riot in Your Throat
publishing fierce, feminist poetry

Jones, Hadley.
1st edition.
ISBN: 979-8-9889898-4-4

Cover Art: Annie Spratt (unsplash.com)
Cover Design: Kirsten Birst
Book Design: Shanna Compton
Author Photo: Rae Martin

Riot in Your Throat
Arlington, VA
www.riotinyourthroat.com

CONTENTS

MARTYR

At 12 years old, I want to die
for Jesus, pray to be like the teenagers
shot in the head for believing in God,
slaughtered for the sake of Christ.

Pastors tell stories of spears and swords
and the jaws of lions. They spell out
in blood: *If you are devoted*
to God, you'll be willing to die.

For the next six years,
my church celebrates
the scripture in my blood.
I speak in the tongues

of church-camp-going, worship-song-singing,
good Christian girl. I love God more
than I love myself. I am
everything they want

until I dive from grace
for a girl whose laugh is sweeter
than the promised land, her touch
as soft as a dove singing me
to safety. I could live
in her arms

if I didn't deserve to die.

I stone my temptation,
my blood a confession—
martyrs go to glory,
queers go to hell.

They told me death
was the holy choice,

so why is my church surprised
when I carve a ladder to heaven

in the skin of my left wrist?
The dead saints at the gate
turn me away, condemn me
to life, and tell me

to pray harder next time.

SAINT

God hasn't heard her prayers
since she was a teenager,

but when she sings
beside me in chapel,

she's a hymnal
without dust,

a melody devoted
to a savior

she has no reason to trust.
I am an out-of-tune piano,

a harmony that rattles,
comes out sharp.

She knows me
as a friend.

Her sister in Christ.
I want to hold her

the way she holds her
coffee at sunrise.

She is the warmth that gets me
out of bed, through the day.

She writes me in journals
while I write her in poems.

For me, she is
every poem.

For her, I am a prayer
that will never be answered.

THE BOYS PLAYED GAMES WHILE WE LEARNED
ABOUT MODESTY

She tells me about the good Christian boys
leering from their legal pads as she debated
foreign policy,

their eyes
riding up her thighs
like drugstore tights.

These boys, named after gospels
and the prophet who tamed lions,
these boys, always on the hunt

for the favor of our mothers,
their bites sharpened by praise
from overprotective fathers.

They take purity vows, win
trophies for the gift of persuasion.
And didn't they earn it?

Parents stay oblivious to the secrets stashed
in church closets, the boys with blazers fastened
by a reputation we can't refute.

They are the boys who played games while we learned
how to follow a dress code that keeps
hemlines at our knees

and sleeves on our shoulders
but can't keep a man from stumbling
when he's already on the prowl.

I cannot argue against the evidence
that every man is hunting, even the ones
who claim to be on my team.

THE ALTARS THEY BUILT

We tape verses to our bathroom mirrors, tattoo them
      over scars. Skip breakfast, not chapel.

We don't need food; we need to be good. They call us good
      when we sing on stage and do not speak

loud enough to be heard outside the confines
      of the girls' dormitories.

They praise our sudden weight loss, the modesty
      that hides our open wounds,

      the silence

that lets boys get away with what we
      would be punished for

      reporting.

      We crawl
to the counseling center
      with a death wish and a plan.

They tell us how to breathe,
      hand us a list of verses calling

death a blessing,
      life a curse.

There is no comfort in Psalms
for girls who slit their wrists.

If we do not bleed all the way
out, we come back to Stockholm,
more liability than student.

We are holier than thou,
never holy enough,

communion wine stains
and biblical names.

On a camping trip with my Christian sorority,
we answer questions

about abuse and suicide
and eating disorders
and self-harm
and rape.

Stand or sit.
Yes or no

to show us we are not
alone. As if that makes it better,
as if that makes it easier.

When asked if we have ever felt
like God could not love or forgive us,
every sister stands up.

This Christian college promised to be home
until we threatened their purity-perfect campus.

They turned
our suffering
into confession.

They tell us our bodies
are evil, nothing but blood
and vomit and sin, but are still

surprised
when we show up
malnourished and bleeding
on the altars they built.

GETHSEMANE

Dim the lights,
change the key.

Inhale fog
and holy water.

I'll drown
my fears

in God's grace.
Every righteous thought
is from God.

Every evil impulse is my
human flesh.

My broken mind
hands down commandments

to tear my car from the road
and rip my body from this earth

like a nail
from the wrist
of Christ.

I have to stop thinking
about death.

Stop feeling sorry
for myself.

I'll lift my hands
until they stop shaking.

There is no anxiety
when Jesus is near.

I guess he couldn't make it
to Sunday service

this time.
Or last time.

I've been waiting
for the smoke to clear,
for the Holy Ghost

to haunt me,
hold me,
heal me.

When all God's children see me sweating
blood on the sanctuary floor,

they call it spiritual anointing.
They don't see the altar

of bathroom tiles stained like glass.
Lord, I will be my own

sacrifice if it means
you will fix me.

Can't you fix me?
What do I need to say
to make you hear me?
Why won't you listen?
What do I need to kill
to make you see me?

If I die,
will I see you?

Will you
take me

home?

TO DIE IS GAIN

When you find
my blood

on the tiles
of your church

tell me how
Christlike I am.

When you find
my body

beneath the spire
of your chapel,

tell them how much
better it is

where I am now, tell them
how much I have

gained.

BAD AGAIN

I hang one leg over the balcony railing.
Forty feet, at least. Maybe fifty. If I search,
How far do you have to fall for it to be fatal?
Google will encourage me to call the lifeline.
I'm no good at estimating distance anyway.

I check the weather instead.
Texas summer never ends,
and I want to shiver. I want
to freeze from something
other than the shoulders

of people who said
they would stay
if I got bad again.
I'm bad again.
No one is here.

I'm still praying to a god
who stopped listening
the first time I pulled this shit.
I ask for help like a prodigal
who was told to leave.

God won't answer, but
campus security picks up
after two rings. Two rings,
and they're on their way.
I failed again.

I am counting the minutes with half my body tethered
to someone else's will for me to live. Later,
a friend says, *I'm so glad you're here,*
I'm so glad you asked for help.
I lie and say, *Me too.*

They promise to stay,
swear on my empty grave,
tell me how much they love me
while I pick out the pills to take
after they leave.

FOUND IN A PRESCHOOL CLASSROOM OR A PSYCH WARD

Coloring books.
An abundance of rainbow
markers—washable,
nontoxic.

Disposable utensils.
Beads ironed into a key chain
for your mother.
Safety scissors.

The kind of scream-crying
one is supposed to
grow out of.
Tissue boxes.

A background-checked adult
hovering in the corner,
wearing a lanyard.

Photos of pets.
Hand-drawn art.
An attempt to run home.
A pack of

crayons. Sidewalk chalk.
Numbers for emergency services.
Instant friendships at a lunch table.
Designated outside time,
snack time, nap time.

Asking for
your mother.

Asking
to go home.

EXIT

Two weeks later, the Benadryl is still on my nightstand.
The bottle rests on top of my spiral notebook collection,
heavy as psych ward furniture. No one checked for danger
in the fourteen days since I left.

The clothes in my closet belong
to the person I was before I got suicidal,
when I only wore shadows.
There is more color in my hamper now.
A button-down shirt covered
in flowers, an oversized sweatshirt
with drawstrings.

The last ones
that haven't been cut.

My door closes
all the way. Privacy,
the first time since admit.

I could strip naked
without someone making notes
of where my scars are
and how many are there?
and why did I do it?
and will I try to do it again?

I could turn on music,
songs with cuss words
and references to sex,

even mentions
of drugs and alcohol.

I could sing.

Instead, I drop the paper sacks
full of my safest belongings.
The brown bags sag on the carpet

like the hair I haven't washed in weeks.
I toss my phone on the bed,
ignoring texts I should respond to.

People love me. They would tell me I could've
talked to them. But I didn't want to kill the mood,
just myself.

Should I stop wearing my seatbelt?
How many milligrams is too many to keep down?
Will anyone speak at my funeral?

I rip months out of my planner. I can't erase the ink,
but I will set my plans on fire,
inhale the smoke and get high
on the disappointment
of people who believed
I was better this time.

My bathroom is full of blood-
stained towels, ripped up promises,
a bathtub deep enough to drown in.

Did your mom take the razors out of the shower?
Are you feeling safe enough to drive yourself home?
Do you know where your dad keeps the gun?

I wash off the smoke breaks and coloring sheets.
Hospital stay number five circles the drain,
threatens to come back up
and flood the house.

I swallow the good pills and throw away
the note left on my childhood bed. I stash
the Benadryl in a bathroom drawer
next to a hollowed-out Band-Aid box,

as if one day, I will forget any
of the plans I've already made.

I know every exit.
The glowing red sign
hangs over my head.

I will always have a way to die.

SIREN

Once, I became an emergency
so he would rescue me.

Now, I become a warning.
Look at what he did to me.
Look at what he does to them.

Don't you believe me?

Don't you believe us?

WHAT I SHOULD'VE TOLD MY COUNSELOR IN OUR LAST SESSION

I wanted to count this in my list of victories.
Graduated from therapy. But I won't graduate
from this school or this therapist.

Do or do not, you repeated.
Do not self-harm, do be mentally
well. I'll commit

to the truth that I am too fucked up for the person
I wrote to with all the rage lowercase letters
could convey: do or do not, there is no

trying to reason with a man
who knows everything
about me. and i know

nothing but destruction. tell me
how to breathe, how to count
backwards by seven until the panic

is easier for you to stomach.
send me back to the line of fire.
All the normal ones can

survive. Why can't you? why can't i
ask one thing of you and expect
a shrapnel of respect?

i scream in the courtroom that sentenced me
out of every plan made to keep me alive.
i scream, and you are the victim

i need to calm down,
take a deep breath,
stop lying about what i said.

i know what i said.
i know what you said
as you ripped the keys from my hand

not to protect me.
to protect your reputation,
your perfect record

of suicidal students who survive
long enough to graduate.
i survived long enough

for you to get tired of my sick.
i told you everything i swore
would stay in my diaries.

maybe it should've burned
like my hands under the faucet
after my sessions with you.

how am i supposed to heal
a wound opened
by a healer?

how can i be honest
when you can't
meet my eyes?

you tell me i am angry. i am
sorry. this is the worst thing
that could've happened to you.

i say i am hurt
and you do not
believe me.

i say i am hurt
and you continue
to hurt me. i crawl

back to your office so you
can mend the flesh broken
by your promises.

i am sorry. you
are happy
to see me.

Will you be coming home soon?
I'd love to meet with you.
We can set up a time next week.

THE LAST THING WE SHARE

Sometimes, I wish I did not write poetry.
Every line reminds me of us,

sitting in your apartment,
reading our words to each other.

Notes app poems about grace and guns,
about the scars we shared.

Never, *I'm sorry,*
always, *Me too.*

I am tired of writing poems
about you instead of with you.

Instead, I write about your handwriting
tattooed on my ribcage, how the ink

bled, and I clutched your
hands. But it was your voice

numbing the needle. Your voice,
the most honest sound

in a sanctuary of lies.
I never told you the truth.

Instead, I wrote another letter.
Sincerely yours, but I

do not know
your address.

I write poems about healing,
as if I can will yours into existence.

I would've held your hands forever
if it meant you couldn't use them
to hurt yourself.

If only it was that easy
for both of us.

Now, you hate poetry.
And I know this is not

the same thing as hating me, but poetry
was the first thing we shared.

A year has passed since the last time
we sat on your couch and read to each other.

I do not know how you are.
You do not know how I am.

This is the last thing we share.

PRAYER OF THE DAMNED

When the rich white pastor on a fifty-foot screen
says victims of abuse become *volunteers*
if they stay, I nearly throw up
both middle fingers, think I might vomit

every swear word I know at this goddamn, motherfucking,
son-of-a-bitch pastor of thirty-thousand people
as we sit in a church with signs that say *Come
As You Are, This is Family, Welcome*

Home, where God is a father
who kicks his queer kids
into the jaws of a noose.
God is a lawyer, asking,

What about the children?
What about your vows?
Why didn't you leave
the first time he hit you?

Here, God throws
the first punch.
Father has to kill Son
just to look at you.

The Almighty Lord sharpens the teeth of lions,
sends them on stage in skinny jeans and wedding rings.
The hip new youth pastor says anxiety is a sin.
The megachurch CEO says gays go to hell.

A sanctuary of lambs cheers them on,
every amen a prayer of the damned.

And I volunteered every Sunday, held doors,
shook hands. They gave me a crown
for praying through the thorns.
I was so good at suffering.

How long did I sit in the front row
an easy target? How much smoke
did I inhale before I decided
I deserved clean air?

I stayed longer than I should have, could've
left the first time a sermon focused
on how great America is.

Or maybe the pastor should've left the first time
he was accused of assault. Maybe their god
should've shut up instead of begging for money
from people desperate for a miracle.

It's a miracle
of the unholy divine
that I dared to leave
at all.

Far from heaven's gates, I thank myself for staying alive
when they wanted me to stay dead. I take the thorn
from my own side and come as I am
to the home I built myself.

BODY SNATCHER

Some days, I am not certain my suicide attempt failed.
The before pictures are of someone I don't recognize.
All her playlists are worship songs; all her friends
are strangers.

I must be some kind of alien.
Snatched her body, cut her hair,
threw her clothes in a bag,
left them to be picked up off the porch

of the house she grew up in.
The house she haunts, lingering in the strangled
notes of a piano, untuned since she learned
what a panic attack is.

I tried to do her justice.
Her clothes seemed to fit
at first. Her friends looked at me
and said her name. I tried
to keep that name alive.

Didn't she have
such a lovely
name?

Those friends are forgetting it now.
They saw the way I took over,
heard her voice
and my words.

They all must hate me
for killing their friend.
For murdering a sister,
daughter, precious girl.

I'm living in her room,
throwing out her favorite books.
I go through her journals,
hunting for my first appearance.

I stole her body,
ripped her out
of the razor-
thin margins
of her diaries.

If she were alive to see me,
she would avoid conversation,
wouldn't want to be under the influence
of the worst kind of sinner:

Unrepentant.
Proud and angry and stuck
in the house she died to leave.

There is still blood pumping through this body.
These bones have yet to break. But something died

on the floor of her roommate's bathroom.
Something died in her car, on the balcony,
on the phone with her therapist.

I wash her down the shower drain,
bury her in the back of her closet,
spread her ashes on piano keys.
Delete her playlists.
Take her life.

She didn't want it
anyway.

FORMAL COMPLAINT

1.

In my dreams, you
apologize. You tell me
how you've changed.

In my days, I still
scan every room I enter,

still feel your hand
around my spine,

still convinced you didn't
mean to hurt me.

2.

In your nightmares,
do I walk into your office

to cough up blood
on your perfect record?

Do you still call yourself
a man of God?

When you see my name
on the formal complaint,

do you even remember
what you did?

HOW DID YOU DO IT

Cornering me at my sister's birthday party,
my aunt asks how I lost
so much weight.

I could say it took years
to find the perfect diet
of satiation and satisfaction,
to forget the difference between
self-control and self-hate.

It was easy, I could say, to drive by
my favorite restaurants without
being stopped by my hunger
when I reminded myself

how many family
have had weight loss surgery.

My siblings look at me
or the floor. My parents
have watched me waste
energy, opening and closing
the fridge until everything inside
grew mold.

My aunt tells me how incredible I am
at disintegrating, barely leaves room
for me to assign credit to my more active job.
See, I wasn't even trying to lose

my will to live. I didn't even notice
the jeans falling from my hips.

I haven't pressed my fingers
between collarbones
or wrapped them around my wrist
or pushed them down my throat—

My aunt tells me
how good I look
as I try to stay standing.

Now, she hands me a slice of cake.
The family gathers round and waits
for me to swallow saccharine shame,

watching me die to become
what they have always
craved.

I STOPPED TAKING CARE OF MYSELF TO SPITE YOU

I cut your words
out of an entire book
of poetry.

Every therapeutic mantra
written on my mirrors
in permanent marker,

crossed out over and over
and over time, I have forgotten
the sound of your

answering machine, left only with the soft
shame of your emails, how you told me
to love myself even when I hate myself.

The ghost of your fingertips
lingers in my open wounds.

You with your saltwater.
Me with my thirst.

I drank
whatever
you prescribed.

I stopped telling the jokes you laughed at.
The coping skills I swore by
sit abandoned in your office,

idle since the last time
you lied to me.

I skip the songs I showed you,
unwrite the poems
you heard first,

run in silence
on the path
you told me
to avoid.

I stay miserable
to spite you.

I count my bones,
my breaths, the milligrams
in a handful—

Is it enough?
Is it too much?
Will I die

in a pool
of my own
vomit

just to prove you
were wrong?

I ran out of victories,
so instead

I count
down the seconds
ticking on the clock
in my new therapist's office.

Even here, even now,
every clock sounds like you
sitting across from me.

Silent.

Staring.

      Waiting

SICK

if i don't admit that i am sick,
no one will be cruel enough
to point it out.

if i admit that i am sick,
no one will be kind enough
to let it slide.

i don't stand a chance
if i can't convince myself.

EVERY AD ON MY PHONE IS FOR EATING DISORDER TREATMENT

in the hallway outside my
treatment center bedroom,
i watch my friends' instagram stories.

a hometown christmas parade,
an ice skating birthday party,

*How healthy is your
relationship to food?*

a pregnancy announcement.

this hour of escapism
cannot help
but be littered with reminders.

*Four ways to set
realistic eating disorder
recovery goals*

one slide offers
a questionnaire
i filled out
six times last month.

Do I have an eating disorder?

as if i hadn't already
memorized the symptoms,
still attempting
to check off each box

to prove i am sick enough
to have something
to recover from.

i came to treatment
willingly.

confessed to my friends.
told my parents.
and still

i am lying
in a bed i made
or the grave i dug
in search of rock bottom.

i thought
when i got here
i would be able
to say the word.

my body
will never
give me
the proof.

how could i be sick

if they take my blood
and it's normal
if they scan my bones
and they're fine

if they weigh me
and nothing

is wrong with me?

even though it feels excessive
to put a second cream in my coffee
or eat more than once a day.

i know an eating disorder
will not bring the satisfaction
i'm looking for.

no one can see the number
of times i've punished myself for being full.
no one else can feel my bones
scrape together when i move

and i'm trying
not to scroll up and down
through old photos.

i'm trying not to watch
the life in my eyes

come back
and leave
and come back
and leave.

some days i wake up
on this hospital mattress

and feel like this is all
an overreaction.

some days i wake up
and only feel
the vacancy
behind my eyes,

the crease between
my best friend's eyebrows
as they took a photo
of my unconvincing smile.

*Are you struggling
with an eating disorder?*

i've never been good
at telling the truth,

*What to say to a friend
struggling with anorexia*

i never asked
to see the photo,

in recovery,
i will look back
at snapshots
of my sickest
thoughts

Five ways to practice
self-compassion

and laugh
at the stretch
of my denial.

i will never be sick enough
to feel worthy of healing.

but one day, may i be
healed enough to know
i always was.

THERE USED TO BE A GIRL HERE

There used to be a girl here;
not made of floral skirts or long hair,
but of trying to be what everyone wanted.

I am lying in her bed, a stranger
she wouldn't live long enough to meet.
I still sing her favorite songs

to a make-believe stadium.
Sometimes, I catch her in the mirror,
still asking, *Are we in the clear yet?*

I have to tell her,
No, and I don't know
what it's like outside these woods.

I don't know if either of us
has been there before.
How do we recover

what we never
had the chance
to lose?

I haven't always wanted to die,
but I've never wanted to live.
But if that girl was here today,

she would see
a shelf of poetry books
like that of the girl she loved.

She would see a flag;
the pride she feared
and yearned for.

She'll find new stuffed animals,
ask for their names. When she finds
two new cats lying beneath my desk,

they will crawl in her lap
and fall asleep. She will laugh
at the inside joke of their names.

When I tell her mine, she will say,
I've never met someone else with my name.
We have to fight to see who keeps it.

And I will let her win.

HEALER

I place my hands over once-red scars
as the saturation fades. After all my wars,
my body paints a white flag.

I have never been broken. I was not born
an incurable sin. My body is the poem;
we are still writing.

If the scars are not scars tomorrow,
I will still have made it this far. My body
is a monument to my own ability to survive.

I made it here. Here,
I become my own
healer.

OCTOBER 19

The concert went late;
we didn't leave early.
12:39 AM, I am in her
third floor apartment

while she holds the puppy
she brought home last month.
He runs around the hardwood floor,
claws tapping as he yaps.

She picks him up. He kisses her
again and again. She almost
drops him, his excitement
too much to contain.

My voice is hoarse
from singing along with her favorite band,
from singing the words to her favorite songs.
String lights are dim and warm and she

is blinding. I capture her smile
in motion. Blurry and brighter
than I've seen her before.
This is my first time

at her new apartment.
She shows me her bed.
Meadow green duvet,
folded weighted blanket.

As she changes into sweatpants 3 sizes too big
and a T-shirt from the school where we met.
She tells me,

I have an extra mattress,
or we could share the bed?

This time, I do not
let myself hesitate.
Let's share the bed.

I cannot close my eyes
the entire night. I keep my hands
to myself. She is a breath away.

If I move,
she will feel
my heartbeat.

If she
moves,
I will take
her hand.

I will bring her palm
against my chest.
I will let my heart
crack under her touch.
I will tell her
the truth.

She doesn't move.
I cannot feel her breathe.

I will never
touch her
again.

HOW TO BURY GRIEF

I have heard a clock ticking in my head
since the day my sister's hamster died.

There was no denial
in my 5-year-old mind,
just a crash course in loss
and regret, just the splinter
of wicker kitchen chairs
against skin that didn't yet know
how to scar.

Death, somehow, was not a new concept.
In my earliest memories, I lull myself to sleep,
not by counting sheep, but by conjuring
the ultimate safety—to be swaddled,
like a beetle in a spider's web.
To be sipped away.

I still hear the clock ticking
on the wall of my childhood
bedroom, inside the steering wheel,
in the bathroom drawer.

I am not afraid of death, simply
aware of its inevitability.
Inescapable yet unpredictable.
We are handed a lifespan
averaged out of a million deaths.

All this time, I have expected *it* to happen to me,
always waiting for the worst-case scenario,
for the accident / illness / natural disaster,
avoiding sleep as if I can avoid it creeping
closer and closer and—

My best friend's dad died
two months ago today.
He had been sick for years,
in and out of the hospital.
But when my friend called,
I was surprised.

The night we buried my sister's hamster
in the box that held my toddler shoes,

I learned how to bury grief.
Which is to say,
I learned how to bury love.

The clock always reminds me:
nothing lasts forever.

We all die
someday.

I have never been afraid of death.
No, it is love that haunts my sleep.
The moment I fall
   my cats snoring at the foot of my bed
   the smell of my mom's morning coffee
   the echoing laughter of a night with friends.

in love is the moment I hear
      it's too late
      shattered glass
      goodbye.
how it ends.

But at the funeral
for my friend's dad,
I could not hear the ticking
over the sound of stifled sobs,
shaking eulogies, and softened
*I love you*s.

No matter how hard I try
to strip life of its meaning,
it always comes
beating back.

I love you
I love you
I love you.

BODY (THE PART OF ME THAT WANTS TO LIVE)

Take the keys to my car,
lock the kitchen drawers.
Tell me to shower. Show me how

to bathe and not draw
shame into flesh, not watch
the last of me stain the tile.

Carry me to the table. Bring
the fork to my lips. I'll bite
with bleeding teeth.

Pour water in my mouth.
I'll take the pills, swallow them
with the threats I didn't mean.

I'm sorry
for every time
I tried to leave you.

I'm sorry
for trying to forget
the pain you can't help

but remember.

While I dream of every overpass
you didn't let me drive off,

you sleep. You wake up,
refuse to leave me
in bed to rot.

The part of me
that wants to live
is you.

It has always
been you.

I FORGIVE THE SCARS FOR HEALING

Having an open wound
does not make me a better person.

Hiding the spilled ink of my pain
does not make me a better friend.

There is no set of before and after pictures
that can show evidence of change.

I forgive the scars for healing.
I do not need to prove myself

to the bathroom mirror—
hasn't it seen enough?

Haven't I shed enough
of my own blood
to know it never could be?

To know I already was?

There are people, now, who know me
not by the degree of my injuries
or the dates of my wounds,

but by the life in my eyes
and the smile I never believed
could belong to me.

I forgive myself for living
long enough to get here.

CASUAL CONVERSATION

My friends stopped shaving
because it's inconvenient
or to make a statement.
I stopped shaving

because I cannot walk through CVS
to pick up the medications
that turn down the volume
of my suicidal thoughts

without stopping to stare at pink packages
of murder weapons, wondering
whether or not I can keep
the blood in my body.

When my coworkers share stories of scars
earned by falling off skateboards,
or making meals for their family,

nobody questions where mine came from.
This is polite and it is obvious

that this isn't a topic for the break room
or the bedroom, or any room without
a licensed professional present.
I tried to make it a joke.
It's so funny how my cat
took a shit on my bed

and my options were to drive myself
to the hospital or to swallow
one thousand milligrams of promises I never
believed I could hold down.

I am just kidding

myself into thinking it's not that serious.
But nobody is laughing. Everyone is
silent while I shout into the microphone
from the balcony railing,

calculating the distance
between my skull and the concrete.
I am funny, I am dying, I am
screaming until this throat

is bloody as murder. Put me
in a crime scene; read every poem
like it's a suicide note. Search for meaning,
find the tape recorder

and listen until you get it,
until you understand
every reason why

and then
take the razors
out of my hand.

Say you will
stay here

and now
and tomorrow
and one year from now

on the 25th birthday I couldn't imagine,
obscure and small and happy
to be there, I will tell you,

The reason I am alive
is that you didn't run
when I wished I wasn't.

When you say, *I love you.*
I'm so glad you're still here.

I will say, *I believe you.*

WHEN ASKED WHERE YOU SEE YOURSELF IN FIVE YEARS

you say nothing. You know
therapists never respond well
when you say, *Hopefully dead.*

If you could see me now, I'm not sure
if you would be more surprised by how
similar or how different we are.

I know you cannot see for yourself,
so let me tell you now:

You didn't dig the grave.
The dirt under your fingernails
came from digging yourself out.

You are not a problem to be solved.

It wasn't your fault.
It was never your fault.
I am sorry he hurt you.

I am sorry you blamed yourself
for trusting him.

You are not broken.
You are a miracle.

You will make it here.
We made it here.

Thank you
for getting help.

Thank you for loving me enough
to live through hell.

And I promise,
I will not leave you behind.

DEVOUT

I kiss Sophie's head outside our church,
blushing pink as a Sunday School valentine.

Mom says, *Don't kiss your friends.* I burn
Baptist-hymnal red. Sophie has a trundle bed,

a swimming pool, eyes bluer
than Noah's flood. She lets me

try on her stick-on earrings.
She's prettier than an Easter dress.

Every girl has a favorite sleepover,
a best best friend. I don't tell her

she is mine.

A gossip of youth group girls swoon
over the ninth grader most likely to become a youth pastor.

Sophie says, *He asked for my number!*
The church parking lot cracks

with jealousy. He gets to text her
at midnight while I tear up

every diary entry from seventh grade
to seventeen,

when the church hallway feels like winter
without snow days. Sophie complains

that she is cold. I hold her hands—
I'll be her softest gloves, the warmest

touch she knows. We play hooky
from youth group, race across the parking lot,

climb into her car and catch our breath.
I'm about to drive away with her

when she drops my hand, uses the warmth
I gave her to wave at her boyfriend.

I want to throw my bible out the window, believe
in her arms instead. But I'm not supposed to dream

about another girl's touch while I sleep
over at her house. I pray myself

awake, stare at her ceiling until
the sun rises on God's wrath.

Maybe I'm dreaming again when Sophie
reaches out and asks, *What's keeping you up?*

I leave the amen in my throat,
take my first honest breath and say,

Let's drive. I take us away
from the pastors who said we'd be damned,

past the billboards advertising hellfire.
I don't need their heaven anymore because Sophie

rolls down the window and laughs loud enough
to drown out the prayers of our parents.

Nobody comes for us.
They're too far gone.

Sophie falls asleep
on my shoulder.

I thank our holy flesh,
kiss her head.

We're too far gone.
We won't go back.

ACKNOWLEDGMENTS

"Bad Again" was published by *Open Minds Quarterly* in 2022.

"Devout" (poem) was published by *Sinister Wisdom* in 2024.

A previous version of "The Last Thing We Share" was published in my 2020 self-published collection *My Therapist Heard It First* under the title "After She Realized I Was Too Much for Her."

THANKS

There's no telling where I'd be if I hadn't had the undying support of my parents. Mom and Dad, thank you for literally flying across the country to keep me safe, for loving my cats almost as much as I do, and for everything else you've done. I couldn't ask for more loving parents. Thank you to my brothers, sister, and sisters-in-law for giving me my sense of humor and taste in media. I would say thank you to Lucie, Phineas, and Lucas, but they are cats who cannot read or appreciate poetry.

Thank you to the friends from my past for making me who I am today. Even if we no longer speak, I will always remember you and the time we spent together. Thank you to Union for making my barista dream come true, giving me the perfect place to write these poems, and being a safe place for the queer community.

To all the gay people in my phone and in real life, this book wouldn't exist without your support. This is for you. You know who you are. I love you. This play is about you.

Thank you so much to Courtney LeBlanc and Riot in Your Throat for hearing my poems and believing in my voice. Additionally, thank you Megan Falley and everyone from Poems That Don't Suck for bringing out the best in my writing.

Lastly, thank you to all the therapists and mental health professionals I've had who have been truly safe and nonjudgmental people who advocated for, believed in, and genuinely cared about me. It means more than you know.

ABOUT THE AUTHOR

Hadley Jones (they/them) is a queer poet from North Texas. They are the author of the poetry collection *My Therapist Heard It First* and the proud parent of three cats. Passionate about letting others know they're not alone in their struggles, Jones writes candidly about queerness, religious trauma, and recovery. You can find them crying over fictional characters at their favorite local coffee shop.

ABOUT THE PRESS

Riot in Your Throat is an independent press that
publishes fierce, feminist poetry.

Support independent authors, artists, and presses.

Visit us online:
www.riotinyourthroat.com

RIOT IN YOUR THROAT BOOKS

Sarah Beddow   *Dispatches from Frontier Schools*
Kathryn Bratt-Pfotenhauer   *Bad Animal*
Kimberly Casey   *Where the Water Begins*
Sonia Greenfield   *All Possible Histories*
Brett Elizabeth Jenkins   *Brilliant Little Body*
Melissa Fite Johnson   *Green*
Melissa Fite Johnson   *Midlife Abecedarian*
Hadley Jones   *Devout*
Hilary King   *Stitched on Me*
Courtney LeBlanc   *Exquisite Bloody, Beating Heart*
Shilo Niziolek   *Little Deaths*
Laura Passin   *Borrowing Your Body*
Sara Quinn Rivara   *Little Beast*
Laurie Rachkus Uttich   *Somewhere, a Woman
  Lowers the Hem of Her Skirt*
Karen J Weyant   *Avoiding the Rapture*

www.ingramcontent.com/pod-product-compliance
Lightning Source LLC
Chambersburg PA
CBHW030512130626
46549CB00007B/2960

9 7 9 8 9 8 8 9 8 9 8 4 4